Cesar Millan

Other books in the People in the News series:

Maya Angelou
Jennifer Aniston
Tyra Banks
David Beckham
Beyoncé
Fidel Castro
Kelly Clarkson
Hillary Clinton
Sean Combs
Miley Cyrus
Ellen Degeneres
Hilary Duff
Zac Efron
Brett Favre
Tina Fey
50 Cent
Al Gore
Tony Hawk
Salma Hayek
LeBron James
Jay-Z
Derek Jeter
Steve Jobs
Dwayne Johnson
Angelina Jolie

Jonas Brothers
Kim Jong Il
Coretta Scott King
Ashton Kutcher
Tobey Maguire
John McCain
Barack Obama
Danica Patrick
Nancy Pelosi
Queen Latifah
Daniel Radcliffe
Condoleezza Rice
Rihanna
Derrick Rose
J.K. Rowling
Shakira
Tupac Shakur
Will Smith
Gwen Stefani
Ben Stiller
Hilary Swank
Justin Timberlake
Usher
Kanye West
Oprah Winfrey

Cesar Millan

by Gail B. Stewart

LUCENT BOOKS
A part of Gale, Cengage Learning

GALE
CENGAGE Learning™

Detroit • New York • San Francisco • New Haven, Conn • Waterville, Maine • London

LIBRARY OF CONGRESS CATALOGING-IN-PUBLICATION DATA

Stewart, Gail B. (Gail Barbara), 1949-
  Cesar Millan / by Gail B. Stewart.
    p. cm. -- (People in the news)
  Includes bibliographical references and index.
  ISBN 978-1-4205-0231-2 (hardcover)
  1. Millan, Cesar--Juvenile literature. 2. Dog trainers--United States--Biography--Juvenile literature. 3. Human-animal communication--Juvenile literature. I. Title.
  SF422.82.M55S74 2010
  636.7092--dc22
  [B]
                                                              2009043642

Lucent Books
27500 Drake Rd.
Farmington Hills, MI 48331

ISBN-13: 978-1-4205-0231-2
ISBN-10: 1-4205-0231-X

Printed in the United States of America
1 2 3 4 5 6 7 14 13 12 11 10

Printed by Bang Printing, Brainerd, MN, 1st Ptg., 04/2010

Contents

F ame and celebrity are alluring. People are drawn to those who walk in fame's spotlight, whether they are known for great accomplishments or for notorious deeds. The lives of the famous pique public interest and attract attention, perhaps because their experiences seem in some ways so different from, yet in other ways so similar to, our own.

Newspapers, magazines, and television regularly capitalize on this fascination with celebrity by running profiles of famous people. For example, television programs such as *Entertainment Tonight* devote all of their programming to stories about entertainment and entertainers. Magazines such as *People* fill their pages with stories of the private lives of famous people. Even newspapers, newsmagazines, and television news frequently delve into the lives of well-known personalities. Despite the number of articles and programs, few provide more than a superficial glimpse at their subjects.

Lucent's People in the News series offers young readers a deeper look into the lives of today's newsmakers, the influences that have shaped them, and the impact they have had in their fields of endeavor and on other people's lives. The subjects of the series hail from many disciplines and walks of life. They include authors, musicians, athletes, political leaders, entertainers, entrepreneurs, and others who have made a mark on modern life and who, in many cases, will continue to do so for years to come.

These biographies are more than factual chronicles. Each book emphasizes the contributions, accomplishments, or deeds that have brought fame or notoriety to the individual and shows how that person has influenced modern life. Authors portray their subjects in a realistic, unsentimental light. For example, Bill Gates—the cofounder and chief executive officer of the software giant Microsoft—has been instrumental in making personal computers the most vital tool of the modern age. Few dispute his business savvy, his perseverance, or his technical expertise, yet critics say he is ruthless in his dealings with competitors and driven more by his desire to maintain Microsoft's dominance in the computer industry than by an interest in furthering technology.

In these books, young readers will encounter inspiring stories about real people who achieved success despite enormous obstacles. Oprah Winfrey—the most powerful, most watched, and wealthiest woman on television today—spent the first six years of her life in the care of her grandparents while her unwed mother sought work and a better life elsewhere. Her adolescence was colored by promiscuity, pregnancy at age fourteen, rape, and sexual abuse.

Each author documents and supports his or her work with an array of primary and secondary source quotations taken from diaries, letters, speeches, and interviews. All quotes are footnoted to show readers exactly how and where biographers derive their information and provide guidance for further research. The quotations enliven the text by giving readers eyewitness views of the life and accomplishments of each person covered in the People in the News series.

In addition, each book in the series includes photographs, annotated bibliographies, timelines, and comprehensive indexes. For both the casual reader and the student researcher, the People in the News series offers insight into the lives of today's newsmakers—people who shape the way we live, work, and play in the modern age.

Needing Help

Suzanne is struggling not to cry. The young woman recently adopted a dog named Opie, a young black Lab mix, from an animal shelter. Suzanne had been excited about bringing him home and giving him a better life. But instead of the happy, friendly dog she had hoped for, Opie has become a nightmare. And the angry red bite marks on her hands tell the story.

The problem, she explains, occurs when they go on walks. The moment Opie sees another dog, he becomes agitated. Barking and straining to get at the other dog, Opie begins writhing and twisting to get off his leash. In frustration, he turns on Suzanne and bites her. In addition to the physical pain, Opie's attacks make her sad, she says, because they show that she and her dog are not working well together. "The episodes are getting worse,"[1] she says, wiping away tears.

"He Would Eventually Harm Our Children"

John and Stella are worried about their dog Coach. For five years the boxer has been a good friend to their young children—especially their son Cade. Recently, however, they have been disturbed by Coach's behavior. The dog has been threatening adults who come to their door, such as the mail carrier and a friend of John's. Even worse, he escaped from the yard and chased a neighbor, who then threatened to sue the family.

Since he was a young boy, Millan always thought he would work with dogs—but not quite on the level he has reached today.

Hoping to find an answer to their problem, John and Stella consulted a veterinarian and other animal experts, all of whom advised them to have Coach euthanized, or killed, before he attacked their children, too. "The impression we got," says John, "was that this was a behavior that couldn't be fixed, and he would eventually harm our children and turn on us."[2]

Heartbroken, the family made arrangements with their veterinarian for Coach to be put down. Stella remembers how sad they all were. "My son Cade wanted to keep some of [Coach's] fur," she says tearfully, "and he wanted us to bring Coach his blanket so Coach could smell him before he died—so he could die in Cade's blanket."[3]

Shiny and Scary

Aggression is the not problem with Kane, a young Great Dane owned by a teacher named Marina. Kane was playing on a shiny linoleum floor when he lost his balance and skidded into a glass door, hurting himself. Since that time, Kane has been fearful of any shiny surface—the kitchen floor, the floor in the veterinarian's office, rain-slicked streets, and worst of all, the floor at the school where Marina teaches.

This makes Marina sad because she has always taken Kane to school with her for special events. Her students love him, and even in the summer when school is not in session, Marina has always felt safer working in the empty building knowing that he was with her. But now, when she tries to bring him into the building and he sees the shiny floor, Kane uses all of his 160-pound body (72.6kg) to pull in the opposite direction. It seems his bad experience has become a phobia, and nothing Marina tries helps him not to be afraid.

Not Doomed

While all of these situations may seem hopeless, Opie, Coach, and Kane are just three of the hundreds of dogs that have been cured of their aggressive or fearful behavior in recent years due to the almost magical ability of one man. He is Cesar Millan, known to television viewers around the world as the "Dog Whisperer."

Millan believes that in almost every instance the dog's owner is at least part of the problem. By working with each of the owners, he was able to produce positive and immediate results in each of the above cases. In Suzanne's case, for example, Millan explained that she was afraid when Opie misbehaved on walks, and the dog could sense her fear. If she could teach herself to be confident and assertive, Opie would sense that, too—and he would be easy to handle. He demonstrated his own confident, calm style, and Suzanne was incredulous as she watched Millan peacefully walk Opie past a pit bull. And Opie did not show any interest in the other dog at all. "It's amazing," she said, laughing. "I cannot believe the change—I can't believe it. He's a different dog!"[4]

And what about Coach, the boxer who was such a threat that experts advised that he be euthanized? Millan was certain that Coach's aggression was fueled by frustration because he spent all his time in the backyard and did not have enough activity. Like many dog owners, this family believed that a spacious yard was enough to keep a dog happy, but Millan explained that was not true. Dogs are migrating animals, he said, and need to be walked regularly—especially a powerful breed such as Coach.

"This is not a dangerous dog," Millan told the visibly relieved family. "This is a dog who is bored."[5] He taught John, Stella, and the children that Coach needed to be walked every day so he had something to do. Within two weeks, Coach was wearing a backpack and carrying Cade's books as they walked to school together.

Kane's story has a happy ending, too. By confidently taking control of Kane and bringing him into the school, Millan was able to prove to the Great Dane that shiny floors were harmless. He explained to Marina that by feeling sorry for her dog's accident on the slippery floor, she was actually encouraging him to be fearful. Dogs, he told her, do not need humans to feel sorry for them. By living in the moment and being confident and strong, she could soon be as successful as he was in walking Kane on those floors. And "soon" is an understatement—the entire rehabilitation process took eleven minutes, after which Marina and even her young son could easily walk him in and out of the school without incident.

Is It Magic?

Who is Cesar Millan, this man who can seemingly change canine behavior at will? For all his skills and talents and knowledge of dog behavior, he has no degree in animal training or veterinary medicine. Born in Mexico, he immigrated illegally to the United States at the age of twenty-one without even a dollar in his pocket. In the nineteen years since then he has become the most famous dog expert in the world.

Not only has he helped celebrities such as Will Smith, Nicolas Cage, and Oprah control their dogs, he has provided inspiration to millions of dog owners around the world who tune in weekly to his highly rated show *The Dog Whisperer with Cesar Millan* on the National Geographic Channel.

Millan's rise to fame is fascinating, as is his uncanny ability to communicate with dogs—an ability he demonstrated even when he was a very young boy.

Chapter 1

El Perrero

Cesar Millan was born on August 27, 1969, in Culiacan, a city in northwestern Mexico, in the state of Sinaloa. Culiacan is about 640 miles (1,030km) from Mexico's capital, Mexico City. But while his family lived in Culiacan, they also spent a great deal of time at his grandfather Teodoro's farm. The farm was located in Ixpalino, about an hour's drive away. Ask him today what part of childhood was the most meaningful, and he will not hesitate to answer. At the farm, he says, "I felt I could really be me, the person I was born to be."[6]

Life on Grandfather's Farm

The farm was not owned by Cesar's grandfather. Rather, he was a *campesino*. Campesinos are workers hired by the wealthy landowners to manage their property and livestock. In return for their work, the campesinos could rent a small parcel of land on which to raise their own food. His grandfather cared for the cattle—walking them down to the stream each day from the pasture and then bringing them back again.

The work was difficult and the conditions almost primitive by American standards. In fact, it was not until about 1981 that the farm got running water and electricity. Before then Cesar's grandmother would walk down to the well each morning with ceramic buckets, pump water into them, and walk back home. "Before she came into the house," recalls Millan, "she would

softly sprinkle some of the water onto the dirt road in front of the doorstep, so the cows wouldn't suffocate us with the dust they churned up as they passed by on their morning parade to the river."[7]

The farm had no television or radio. He recalls that "once the sky turned dim in the evenings, there was little for us kids to do in the candlelight. While the adults talked softly into the night, my older sister and I would try to drift off to sleep in the stifling heat."[8] But Cesar's mornings were always fun.

Watching the Animals

The best part of life on the farm was to be around a variety of animals. Young Cesar could not wait to get out of bed each morning just to be near them. He spent the day walking among

Millan's grandfather was a campesino, like the one pictured here, who managed a farmer's livestock and lived on his farm. Millan has said that his time on his grandfather's farm was the most meaningful part of his childhood.

them, watching them, trying to understand how their minds worked and how they communicated with one another. His mother, he says, still reminds him that from the time he was old enough to touch any of those animals, he could never learn enough about them:

> Whether it was a cat, a chicken, a bull, or a goat, I wanted to know what the world looked like through the eyes of each animal—and I wanted to understand that animal from the inside out. I never thought of them as the same as

us, but I can't remember thinking that animals were "less" than us, either. I was always endlessly fascinated—and delighted—by our differences.[9]

But as fascinating as all the animals were, no species was as interesting to Cesar as the dogs on the farm. Those dogs, and the lessons Cesar learned about them from his grandfather Teodoro, provided the foundation for his own ideas about dog behavior.

Lessons from Farm Dogs

The dogs on the farm were not wild, nor were they pets, but rather were something in between. They ran together in packs, or groups, of between five and seven. They were mixed-breed dogs. Millan remembers them as working dogs, always running alongside his grandfather as he herded the cows down to the stream. They did not come indoors, but they were still consid-

The dogs on the farm, and the lessons Millan learned about them from his grandfather, provided the foundation for his own ideas about dog behavior.

ered part of the farm family because of their loyalty and the protection they provided.

For example, Millan remembers that when his grandmother was carrying food out for the workers, a dog would always walk beside her "lest an aggressive pig appeared to try to take the food away from her."[10] And if one of the workers left a hat out in the field, one of the dogs would always stay back until that worker came back for it.

Those dogs just seemed to know how to do those things. Years later, Millan began to wonder how the dogs knew to act the way they did. Why were they so loyal and helpful, when some other farm dogs were not? His grandfather had never trained the dogs. They looked after themselves—even scavenging or hunting for their own food—and they were not rewarded with dog biscuits or other treats. Yet for some reason, Millan says, the dogs never growled at any of the humans—including the young children. They never fought among themselves, as other packs of dogs did on other farms.

Advice for a Lifetime

Millan believes that the dogs acted the way they did because they sensed who the leader was—his grandfather. It was his energy—that calm, even-tempered demeanor—that made the dogs understand that he was in charge. He never lavished praise on them, nor did he ever hit or abuse them. He was simply the leader, and all of the dogs knew it, says Millan.

> I realize now that this was because my grandfather never let any dog take the leadership role away from him—or from the rest of us humans, for that matter. He instinctively understood that for the dogs to live in harmony with us— to work willingly with us on the farm and never show aggression or dominance toward us—they all needed to understand that we humans were their pack leaders.[11]

As a child, Cesar learned from his grandfather that training a dog was all about understanding the nature of a dog and its need to follow a leader who is confident—whether that leader is a dog or a person. He says that his grandfather knew that Cesar, even as a young child, understood that. "I think he recognized that of all his grandkids, I was the one born with that same special gift," Millan writes in his book *Cesar's Way*. "The wisest thing he ever said to me was, 'Never work against Mother Nature. You only succeed when you work *with* her.'"[12]

Moving to Mazatlan

As Cesar continued to enjoy life on the farm, his father was concerned about his children's lack of education there. Though occasional teachers were sent out to the rural areas to work with farm children, it was not like attending a real school. The teachers did not show up every day, and as a result, the children's schoolwork suffered. So when Cesar was six years old, the family moved to the coastal city of Mazatlan, a city much larger than Culiacan, where he grew up.

But while the schools in his new home were good, Cesar was unhappy. Life in this bustling city was a more indoor existence than he would have liked, he remembers:

> On the farm, I could go outside for hours and hours, walking the land, following "the guys"—my father or my grandfather or the other ranch hands—and always with the dogs trailing behind us. There wasn't anywhere I couldn't go on foot. Now, my mom was nervous about only letting us walk to the corner and back. . . . The only time I felt "free" again was on the weekends when we'd go back to the farm. But those weekends never seemed to last long enough.[13]

Different Dogs

When he did venture outside in the city, Cesar was shocked at the difference between the dogs in Mazatlan and the farm dogs he had grown to love. The city dogs were not nearly as scrawny—probably because they were able to scavenge from so many more garbage cans. However, it was not their physical differences that bothered him but rather the way they were treated.

Millan was shocked at the difference between the dogs in Mazatlan and the farm dogs with which he grew up. Dogs in the city were the object of people's anger.

For the first time in his life, Cesar saw dogs being threatened and abused by humans. Of course, in the country a farmer would drive a dog off for killing chickens or for causing other problems. But in the city the dogs seemed to be the object of people's anger just for existing. "I witnessed people throwing rocks at dogs and swearing at them, even if the dogs were only passing by their car or running past their store or fruit stand," he recalls. "It tore me up inside just to see that."[14]

Largely because of the ugly life those city dogs led, Cesar—who had always loved watching dogs—made a decision to stop studying them. "That was the only time in my life," he recalls, "when I actually detached myself from dogs. I think in some ways, that's when I became detached from myself."[15]

Not Fitting In

The detachment that Cesar experienced was apparent in several ways. He occasionally lashed out at his parents because he was unhappy—something he had never done before. He became lonely. He did not form any strong friendships with his classmates or neighbors. He explains that he did not seem to fit in with city kids his own age. "From day one, it was clear to me that how they felt about their lives had nothing to do with how I felt about mine," he says. "I didn't make any judgment about better or worse; I just sensed that there was really not that much we had in common."[16]

But he knew that it would not be wise to isolate himself, to shrug off a social life. "I realized that if I was going to make it in the city, somebody needed to change his behavior, and it obviously wasn't going to be the other kids. They were the 'pack,' so I tried to adapt and fit in."[17]

He did try hanging out with them, swimming (Mazatlan is a beautiful coastal city with great beaches) and playing soccer and baseball. But deep inside, he says, he knew he was faking it: "It was never like on the farm, chasing a frog here and there, catching fireflies in jars and then setting them free, or simply sitting under the stars, listening to the crickets' song. Nature had always offered me something new to learn, something to think about. Sports were just working off energy and trying to fit in."[18]

Judo and Joaquim

But while Cesar did not want to be in the city, he did have some positive experiences during that time. One was his introduction to judo, a Japanese form of martial arts. Soon after arriving in Mazatlan, his parents were aware of their young son's anger. They were aware, too, that his anger would cause him to have a much harder time adjusting to his new life. It would be better, they thought, to let him act out his aggression by learning judo rather than by arguing with them and fighting with his sisters.

Judo is more than a method of self-protection. The central idea of judo is to use an opponent's strength and size to one's own advantage. For example, a small man who is about to be pushed by a larger man could use quickness and control to step smoothly out of the way, then trip the larger man as his momentum carries him forward. By not throwing a punch, the small man can defeat a much larger one. Judo's central philosophy is that a person should work with nature, using the natural attributes he or she has, rather than against nature—an idea that sounded to Cesar very much like his grandfather's view of how dogs should be treated.

The judo master at the studio was a man named Joaquim, who had studied judo for many years. Joaquim took an interest in the troubled boy, realizing that he was interested in more than just the physical side of judo. He talked to Cesar about Japanese culture and the Japanese concept of nature—the need to have harmony between the body and the mind.

Cesar was fascinated and realized that Joaquim and his grandfather were very much alike in their ideas—something that must have been comforting for the boy who missed life on the farm. Cesar was interested in exploring some of the other aspects of judo, too. For example, he learned meditation and breathing techniques to calm and steady the mind. He also learned how to focus his mind on goals that he might set for himself—techniques, he says today, that have helped him immeasurably in his work: "Many of the techniques I learned in judo—single-mindedness, self-control, quieting the mind, deep concentration—are skills I still use every day, and find especially crucial in my work with

Millan's parents encouraged him to learn judo as a way to deal with his aggressive behavior. Millan was drawn to judo's concept of having harmony between body and mind.

dangerous, red-zone aggressive dogs," he says, adding, "My parents couldn't have found a more perfect outlet for me during that phase of my life."[19]

"He Looked at Me as if I Were Crazy"

Perhaps the most exciting thing that happened to him during his time in the city was spotting a purebred dog—the first he had ever seen. It was an Irish setter, owned by a man named Dr. Fisher. Cesar was astonished at how different the dog looked from the scruffy, mistreated packs of dogs that roamed the city. He admired how sleek and shiny her red coat was. "I fell in love," he remembers. "Every time I saw the man walk by with this dog, I fell in love all over again. I just thought, 'Oh, man, I've got to have that beautiful dog.'"[20]

He followed the man home to find out where he lived. From that day on, Cesar was like a shadow, following the man and his dog as they took their daily stroll around the neighborhood. One day he

Purebred, Mixed Breed?

Millan was excited about receiving the Irish setter puppy Saluki when he was a boy. Saluki's mother was the first purebred dog he had ever seen, and he says that owning a purebred dog taught him a lesson that has been important in his work. "Purebred or mutt, farm dog or house dog, Siberian husky, German shepherd or Irish setter, a purebred is first and foremost just an ordinary dog in a designer suit. . . . I think too many people blame 'breed' for their dogs' problem behavior," he says. "Sweet Saluki taught me that beautiful purebred dogs and funny-looking mutts are both the same thing under their skin—they are both simply *dogs first*."

Cesar Millan, *Cesar's Way*. New York: Harmony, 2006, p. 32.

learned that the dog had had a litter of puppies, Cesar remembers, and that was when he took a brave step. He introduced himself to Fisher and asked him if he might have one of those puppies.

"He looked at me as if I were crazy," Millan recalls. "There I was, some stranger, a kid, and I wanted him to give me a valuable purebred puppy, which rich people might pay hundreds of dollars for. Still, I think he could read in my eyes how serious I was about it. I really wanted one of those dogs!"[21]

Saluki, Who Was Not a Saluki

He did not give Cesar a puppy that day. But a few years later, to Cesar's great delight, he did give him a puppy from one of his dog's litters. How does he explain Fisher's generosity toward a boy he hardly knew? "My perseverance was pretty strong," he says. "He saw me many, many years. When he finally gave me the dog, he said, 'You've been waiting a long time, right?'"[22]

The puppy was a beautiful Irish setter—not with the classic thin body but stockier. Cesar named her Saluki, and she was his good, loyal companion for nearly ten years. In a recent interview he explained why he chose that name:

> Saluki is actually the name of a breed of dogs, a very ancient breed from Egypt. I knew that because my father eventually learned that the best present for me wasn't a toy car or something like that. It was a dog book—I really enjoyed reading about dogs. He once gave me a beautiful encyclopedia of dog breeds, and I loved reading about the different kinds of dogs I'd never seen or heard of. Anyway, when I got this puppy, I guess I figured if I couldn't have a Saluki, I'd at least have a dog with that name.[23]

While he enjoyed having his own dog, Cesar was still restless. When he turned fourteen, the family moved again. They were still in Mazatlan, but because his father had landed a better job, they moved to a nicer neighborhood—and into a house rather than a crowded apartment. He was more comfortable but still unsure about the future—especially when his friends talked about what they wanted to do when they grew up.

The first purebred dog that Millan had ever seen was an Irish setter. Dr. Fisher, who owned the dog, gave Millan a puppy from one of his dog's litters.

How Dogs Learn Danger

In his book *Cesar's Way*, Millan remembers watching the dogs on his grandfather's farm as he struggled to understand how dogs learn basic survival skills. One of his memories involves watching puppies explore a dangerous scorpion.

They obviously were fascinated by this outlandish creature, and they inched toward it tentatively, leading with their noses. As soon as they got close, the scorpion started to move toward them, and the puppies jumped back. Then the puppies began sniffing around the scorpion all over again, then backed off, then started again—but never got so close as to get stung by it.

How did they know how far they could go? Was the scorpion sending them "signals" as to what its boundaries were? How did those two pups sense the scorpion's poison? I witnessed the same things with one of our other dogs and a rattlesnake. Did she smell danger from the rattlesnake? I knew the way I had been taught that an animal was poisonous. My father told me, "You go near that scorpion, and I'm going to spank you." . . . But you never saw a dog father or dog mother telling a pup, "This is how it is."

Cesar Millan, *Cesar's Way*. New York: Harmony, 2006, pp. 26–27.

Millan shares many stories of growing up on his grandfather's farm in his book Cesar's Way.

"I didn't feel the desire to be a fireman, or a doctor or a lawyer or anything like that," he says. "I didn't know exactly what it was I'd be doing, but I knew that if there was a profession that involved dogs, I wanted to be part of it."[24]

By the time he began high school, Cesar started to realize what it was he wanted to do. An idea was beginning to hatch in his mind, but he was not ready to talk about it. At least, not yet.

Chapter 2

Beginnings of a Dream

Though Cesar knew that he wanted to work with dogs in some way, he was not yet certain how. But one idea kept coming back into his mind—an idea that had occurred to him years before, when he was very young. The idea actually began with two American television shows.

"What a Feat!"

Both shows had dogs as their central characters. The first was *Lassie*, which featured a farm boy named Timmy and his beautiful collie. *Lassie* was popular in the United States and was broadcast in Mexico, dubbed in Spanish. Lassie was very smart and seemed to always know when Timmy or someone in the family needed help.

The second show was called *The Adventures of Rin Tin Tin*. Also dubbed in Spanish, the show was about a young orphan named Rusty who had been adopted by a cavalry outpost in the American West. Rusty's dog was a German shepherd named Rin Tin Tin, or "Rinty." Like Lassie, Rinty was smart and brave and saved Rusty (and the cavalry, sometimes) from dangers.

When he was young, Cesar was enthralled with the adventures, even though he later realized that the stories could not have been true:

> I knew that of course Lassie didn't really understand the words that Timmy was saying. I also figured out that normal

Millan was fascinated with the television show Lassie as a young boy. It helped him further realize his goal of wanting to work with dogs.

dogs didn't automatically do the heroic things that Lassie and Rin Tin Tin did every week. Once I learned that trainers stood offscreen, controlling the dogs' behavior, I began to romanticize them. What a feat, to turn those ordinary dogs into such stellar actors![25]

"The Only Thing You Hear Is Hollywood and Disneyland"

Cesar's idea, which he had not shared with anyone, was to become one of those dog trainers. He would go to Hollywood, where all the movies and television shows were filmed, and get a job working with dogs on camera.

He knew then, Millan remembers, that he wanted to go to the United States. "Where I'm from," he says, "the only thing you hear is Hollywood and Disneyland. You don't hear Texas, you don't hear Ohio, you don't even hear New York. My target was Hollywood, because that was the only thing I knew."[26]

He began saying his goal out loud over and over to himself. Just doing that made him feel hopeful and strong and on the correct path. It was, he remembers, "like being given a glass of water after nearly dying of thirst."[27] And when he was comfortable with it, he decided to say it to someone else—his mother.

"I'm Very Symbolic"

He remembers that he was thirteen years old and on his way to a judo tournament. He and his mother were sitting in front of a big statue in the city, and he said, "Mom, I am going to be the best dog trainer in the world!"[28] He remembers the day fondly, for he got just what he expected from her—total support. When he asked if she thought it was possible, she replied, "Of course, *mi amor* [my love]! You can be whatever you want!"[29]

Millan says revealing his dream was such a momentous occasion that he takes his mother to that same spot every time he goes back to Mazatlan to see his family. "All the time," he says.

"I'm very symbolic. As soon as I [arrive] . . . I get my mom, and we go to that spot. Just to express my gratitude."[30]

As exciting as that moment was, however, he was only thirteen years old and years away from being able to venture off to the United States and be taken seriously as a dog trainer. But he could do something, and it was something he still enjoys today. "I made plans," he says. "I love it, mapping it out, thinking about what I could do, how it would work. I still do it now, in the afternoons. There's just something pleasurable about thinking about the future like that."[31]

El Perrero

The first step in reaching his dream, he decided, was to get a part-time job in a local veterinarian's office, which he did as soon as he turned fifteen. This veterinarian's office was not fancy. It was a combination medical clinic, dog grooming facility, and boarding kennel. But Cesar did not care. He was working with dogs, and that was all that mattered.

At first he was a sort of janitor—sweeping the floor, emptying the garbage, and cleaning up after the animals. But soon it was evident to the veterinarian's staff that he had an uncanny ability to work with the most frightened or aggressive dogs, calming them merely by his presence. As a result, he was soon promoted to groomer, and then vet technician—someone who would work alongside the vet while a dog received medical care. When a dog needed surgery, Cesar's job was to clip or bathe the part of the body to be operated on and then help bandage the wound after surgery.

As the years went by, he continued to enjoy his job. However, he realized that many of his peers thought it very odd that he would want to spend his days working with dogs. They began calling him *el perrero*, "the dog boy." "Remember," he says, "in the city of Mazatlan, this wasn't exactly a compliment. . . . In Mexico . . . dogs in the city were considered lowly, dirty beasts—and because I hung around with dogs, I was, too, by association. Did I care? No. I was on a mission."[32]

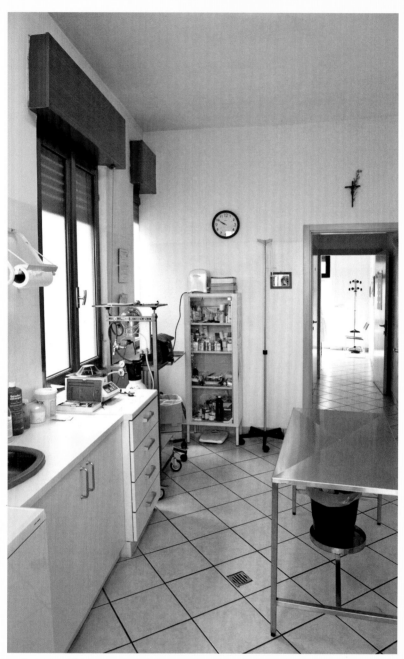

When Millan turned fifteen, he got a part-time job in a veterinary clinic, working his way up from janitor to vet technician.

"I Can't Explain It"

Finally, when he was twenty-one years old, Cesar decided to follow the dream he had had since he was a boy. On December 23, 1990, he went to his mother and told her he was leaving. Although she had always supported him, she was upset. She told him he was crazy, that it was just two days until Christmas. Even more troubling, she said, was that they had only one hundred dollars to give him—not nearly enough to get across the border.

As an adult, Millan has been honest about coming to the United States illegally. He explains that it is virtually impossible for most poor Mexicans to get a legal visa, for it requires expensive payoffs to government officials. "The Mexican government is about who you know and how much money you have," he says. "You have to pay enormous amounts to officials in order to get a legal visa. My family had no way to get their hands on that amount of money."[33]

So like millions of Mexican people before him, he decided to cross the border illegally—without a visa—hoping that *la Migra*, or U.S. border patrol agents, would not catch him and send him back. Thinking about what lay before him was a little intimidating and exciting at the same time, he recalls:

> I was going alone, just by myself. And the language was a problem, because I didn't speak any English at all. You know, you get so conditioned to having your mom and dad to protect you, to tell you right from wrong. And you're in a territory that none of your family members have been in, so you have no feedback, no advice from anyone. You just go, and believe that God has a plan for you.[34]

"I Saw Some Terrible Things There"

Cesar knew that Tijuana was a popular crossing place, so he set out on the long trip from Mazatlan. Tijuana was, and is today, a very dangerous place. Violent gangs and dangerous drug dealers think nothing of killing innocent people. The city is filled

U.S. Border Patrol monitors the Mexico-U.S. border in Tijuana, making it difficult and dangerous for illegal immigrants to enter the United States.

with hundreds of desperate people waiting to get across the border into the United States—either to find work or to reunite with loved ones who have already crossed. And smugglers promise to take them there.

These smugglers, known as coyotes, often prey upon the people who hire them to cross the border. Some demand their payment—sometimes thousands of dollars—while still in Mexico, rather than collecting it when they reach their destination. Once they reach the desert, some unscrupulous coyotes simply abandon the people, leaving families—many of them carrying small children—to get lost in the desert where some die from the heat or lack of water. It was an eye-opening experience for the young man from Mazatlan. "I saw some terrible things there," he says. "I saw a lot of people dying, a lot of people suffering while I was on the border."[35]

Cesar was concerned about money. He had only the one hundred dollars his parents gave him, and he was reluctant to hand it over to one of the coyotes to get him across the border. But after trying—and failing—three times to cross the border by himself, he was beginning to realize that getting to the United States was much more difficult than he had thought.

"Not One Drop of Fear"

One rainy night, two weeks after arriving in Tijuana, Cesar was preparing to try a fourth time. As he was standing outside by a coffee stand, a young coyote walked up to him and asked if he wanted to cross. When the man offered to take him across for only one hundred dollars, Cesar agreed. But the coyote insisted that they go to a safer place to cross than Tijuana. He told Cesar that they should double back toward the east, away from Tijuana. That same night, they began the journey.

They ran through the dark until Cesar was exhausted. Then the coyote pointed out the lights of *la Migra* just to the north. He told Cesar that before they could cross they would have to hide silently in a muddy water hole until the border patrol officers moved away. It was a very long wait in water that was chest high, Cesar remembers, but he was not frightened.

Although he was trembling with cold and tired beyond belief, Cesar says he felt no fear at all. "It's unbelievable," he says, but not one drop of fear came to me. I was not afraid whatsoever. Just the feeling of 'this is what I need to do.' I was in the water for more than four hours. . . . I felt that somebody was taking care of me."[36]

Finally, as the red lights in the distance moved away, the coyote told him they had to move quickly. They ran north, crossing through a junkyard, a freeway, and down into a tunnel. After running through the tunnel, they came to a gas station, where the coyote gave twenty dollars to a taxi driver, who took Cesar into San Diego.

He had done it—arrived in the United States. As he writes in *Cesar's Way*, "[The taxi driver] drove me to San Diego and dropped me off there—dripping wet, thirsty, hungry, my boots covered with mud. I was the happiest man in the world. I was in the U.S."[37]

On the Streets

By crossing the border into the United States, Cesar had taken a step toward his dream of becoming a Hollywood dog trainer. However, he faced immediate challenges, such as how to live when he had no contacts, no home, and no money. Even though Hollywood was only about 150 miles from San Diego, it felt a million miles away.

He knew his next step was to make some money. He wanted to find a job, but because he could not read or speak English, he could not use the newspaper's classified ads or the yellow pages. In fact, the only English he had learned was the question, "Do you have a job application?"

During his first weeks in San Diego, he had no luck at all. He lived on the streets, still in the same clothes he wore when he crossed the border. Then one day he saw a sign with an image he recognized—a dog-grooming business. He walked in and asked if they had any work for him. To his amazement, the answer this time was "yes."

"I Felt Like a Tourist"

In an interview with Mary-Jo Dionne of *Modern Dog Magazine*, Millan talks about the time he first arrived in the United States. Dionne asks if he was homeless at that time.

> For two months. But the way I looked at it was that I was a tourist. When people ask me what it is I like about America, to me, it's the beautiful freeways. Plants in the middle of the road, well-groomed. I'd never seen that. And so to me, I felt like a tourist, not an illegal guy running from anything. No place to live, no money. But I never begged; I worked. At 7/11 you could get two hot dogs for 99 cents. So it was enough. One of the things I always wanted to drink was soda. My mom did not allow us to drink soda. And here, you get refills! For $1.69, you can get all the soda you want!

Quoted in Mary-Jo Dionne, "Cesar Millan: The Man Behind the Whisper," *Modern Dog Magazine*. www.moderndogmagazine.com/articles/cesar_millan/755.

On the Job

The grooming shop was owned by two women who were willing to give him a try. As did most groomers, they had trouble with anxious or aggressive dogs who did not want any part of the grooming process. The women gave Cesar a chance to take on a cocker spaniel as his first customer.

Using the same energy and demeanor he had used when dealing with the dogs on his grandfather's farm, he easily calmed the nervous spaniel. He quickly did the grooming as the two women looked on, amazed at what this young Mexican man could do. They paid him half of the fee they charged for grooming that dog, and Cesar was astonished to receive thirty dollars. "I couldn't believe it," he said later. "I bought jeans and a shirt. I'd been wearing the same shirt for two months."[38]

"It's Like Cowboys"

Though he sometimes works with what he calls "red-zone" cases—dogs that are so unbalanced that they would attack a human or another dog—Millan tells *New York Times* reporter Edward Wyatt that one of the most important advantages he has over them is that he is not afraid.

> It's like cowboys. They grow up around the horse and the cow; they are not afraid of them. You can be a huge dog lover, you can have a passion for it, but that doesn't mean you can develop the strong assertive state of mind that is required to be around hard-core cases. These cases I work with, they are coming after me. But I don't develop fear. Like the people who work around cobras—they don't have fear in their mind. What makes you become a pack leader is being in a calm assertive state 100 percent of the time.

Quoted in Edward Wyatt, "A 'Whisperer' Howl of Triumph, from the Curb Up," *New York Times*, May 23, 2006.

Cesar was hired on the spot. Not only did he get half of the fee for each dog he groomed, the owners of the shop also offered to let him sleep on the premises. He was grateful for the work, especially because it was with dogs. "They gave me all the cocker spaniels, all the poodles, all the terriers, all the hard-to-groom dogs—which happened to be the dogs for whose grooming people paid the most," he says. "The shop charged $120 for an average poodle—which meant $60 for me!"[39]

Noticing a Difference

Though he had a steady job and a free place to sleep, Cesar was frugal with his money. Breakfast and dinner consisted of hot dogs (two for ninety-nine cents) from a nearby convenience store. He had no car, no expensive hobbies. His needs were simple,

Millan's first job in San Diego was at a dog groomer, where he was given all the difficult dogs to work on. His first was a cocker spaniel.

Millan always had a special talent for noticing differences in dogs' behaviors, and now he shares his talent by speaking in front of huge audiences.

and he was happy to save almost every dollar he earned. His goal was still uppermost in his mind, and he knew he would need money to move to Los Angeles and pursue his dream.

His new job also gave him the opportunity to notice some real differences between the dogs he knew in Mexico and those he was seeing in California. Certainly, the physical differences were great. "During my time at the groomer's," he remembers, "I saw the most beautiful dogs I had ever imagined—stunning examples of their breeds, with clear eyes, gleaming coats, and healthy, well-fed bodies."[40]

However, he also noticed that the dogs he saw were often quite unbalanced. Their mental health did not match up with their physical beauty. While the dogs he had known on his grandfather's farm were scruffy and as far from a pedigree as one could find, they were happy and content. They got along with people as well as with one another. But these American dogs were nothing like that, as he later explained:

> Growing up with animals, you can automatically sense when their energy levels are normal. That healthy, balanced state of mind is recognizable in any creature—it's the same for a horse, a chicken, a camel, even for a child. Yet I could see right away that these American dogs were exhibiting what seemed to me to be a very strange, very unnatural energy. Even at the vet's in Mazatlan, I had never encountered dogs that were so neurotic, so excitable, so fearful and tense."[41]

Interestingly, as Cesar adapted to life in California, his observations about the dogs he worked with would have an influence on his goals. Though he did not realize it at the time, his dream was evolving. And it was a dream that was going to strike a chord with dog owners throughout the world.

Chapter 3

Breaking Away

By the end of his first year in San Diego, Millan had saved enough money to move to Los Angeles. He was very grateful to the two women who had hired him to work in their grooming business. In his acknowledgements at the beginning of *Cesar's Way*, he thanks them, calling them his American guardian angels. "Forgive me for not recalling your names—I knew no English then, and American names were very difficult for me," he writes. "But if you are reading this, please know that I'll never forget what you did for me."[42]

Kennel Boy

Millan was a determined young man, and he knew it was time to take the next step toward his goal. He wanted to become a dog trainer, and he was excited to get a job at what many said was one of the best dog training facilities in Los Angeles. Customers would drop their dogs off for a two-week stay to master the basic commands of sit, stay, come, and heel.

Millan was one of the kennel boys who locked each dog in its individual cage until it was time for its training session. He brought the dog to the trainer at the prescribed time and then returned the dog to the cage. While he did no training, he was hoping to learn by watching what the trainers did.

But what he saw alarmed him. A large number of these dogs, though physically healthy, were very unbalanced. They were fearful and anxious, and Millan believed the training facility was actually making them worse. Because they were caged separately, many of the dogs were anxious and lonely. Also, because this business guaranteed success in training a dog by the end of the two-week period, the trainers often resorted to harsher methods to make the dogs obey. Though the methods were not cruel, he remembers, they made the dogs even more fearful.

"I witnessed dogs respond obediently to a trainer's commands," he says, "while crouched down, ears back, cowering, tail between the legs—body language that broadcasts loud and clear, 'I'm only obeying you because I'm terrified.'"[43]

His Own Way

At this facility, the problems were usually among the strong breeds with reputations of being dangerous and aggressive, such as pit bulls, rottweilers, and German shepherds. But while the other kennel boys would yell at a dog that exhibited fear or aggression, Millan had his own system.

"I'd approach [the frightened or aggressive dog] silently," he explains. "No talk, no touch, no eye contact. In fact, when I saw such a dog, I'd open the gate, then turn my back as if I were about to walk off in the other direction. Eventually, since dogs are naturally curious, the dog would come to me."[44]

His method worked well. Once the dog approached him, he could easily put a leash on it, because the dog was no longer frightened. It accepted him as the one in charge, just as a dog in a pack would submit to a confident (but not aggressive) leader. It occurred to him that he was actually applying the lessons he had learned as a small boy on the farm. His grandfather's words, "Never work against Mother Nature," seemed to be the key. "This was the birth of the rehabilitation methods I still use today," says Millan, "although I couldn't have explained in words what I was doing at the time—neither in English nor in Spanish. Everything I did just came instinctually to me."[45]

Millan always had a special talent for dealing with difficult and aggressive breeds, such as German shepherds.

The Power of the Pack

As the months went by, he gained a reputation similar to the one he developed as a dog groomer in San Diego. Far from being intimidated by a snarling Rottweiler or an angry pit bull, he was calm and comfortable around them, and they with him. A dog's anxiety seemed to melt away as Millan quietly snapped a leash on the dog and took it to a training session or for a bit of exercise around the grounds.

One thing he did caused some nervousness among the managers of the facility. "One day, I went out into the yard holding two Rottweilers, a shepherd, and a pit bull all at once," he recalls. "I was the only one there who had ever attempted anything like this. Most of the other employees thought I was crazy."[46]

Quite by accident, however, he began to realize that a group of calm and balanced dogs could actually help create that sense of calm in a nervous or unbalanced dog. As long as he was careful about watching for any aggressive behavior among the pack, the new dog would eventually calm down to fit into the group. He sensed that this was an important lesson—one that would also become an important part of his dog rehabilitation business in the coming years: Dogs can heal one another, for there is power in the pack. Once again, it seemed clear to him that working with Mother Nature seemed to be the simplest and best answer to a dog's problems.

An Offer

One of the people who noticed his talents was a client whose golden retriever had benefited from the training facility. The man noticed that Millan was an exceptionally hard worker but that he seemed unhappy. He asked Millan if he would like to come work for him. "I asked him what I would be doing for him," Millan recalls, "thinking of course that it would have something to do with dogs. I was a little let down when he said, 'You'd be washing limousines. I own a fleet of them.'"[47]

At first he was going to decline the offer; however, as he thought more about it, he realized he knew nothing about running a business. This man was confident and knew what he was doing. Deciding that he could learn something that would help him later in his training business, Millan accepted and began the new job.

Looking back, he says that he was a perfectionist with any job he was ever given, and this one was no different. He was always anxious to prove both to his boss and to himself that he could do a job well. "I was a good car-wash guy," he says. "I could clean thirteen limousines a day. I had the drive. I didn't care what I was doing, if I was a kennel guy or a guy washing cars, I wanted to be the best."[48]

One of the perks of the job was his own car—something he had never had. It was a white 1988 Chevy Astro van, and it was a red-letter day when his boss presented it to him. That car gave him a sense of freedom in a city where driving is almost a requirement for getting around. The day he received it was also the day he decided that he would start his own business on his off hours.

Shifting Gears

The business, which he named Pacific Point Canine Academy, was not a dog training venture. He had been thinking hard about his childhood dream of being the best dog trainer in the world. But since crossing the border from Mexico, Millan's dream had slowly begun to evolve. He realized that dogs in the United States desperately needed something, but it was not training. It was rehabilitation.

So many American dogs seemed to be leading unhappy lives, filled with fear and anxiety. And that fear made them unruly and hard for their owners to handle. Millan remembers being concerned that unless those dogs could become more stable and balanced, their owners would get frustrated and take them to shelters, where the dogs would be euthanized.

He realized that rehabilitating these dogs was a far more important goal than simply training dogs to sit, roll over, and heel. Energized by his discovery, he created a design for the Pacific Point Canine Academy and had a jacket made for himself with

Millan saw that many American dogs were leading unhappy lives in shelters, and felt they needed to be rehabilitated rather than euthanized.

the academy's design emblazoned on the back. Somehow, he decided, he would use the hours he was not cleaning limousines to work with troubled dogs. And hopefully, even though he had no money to advertise, he could grow this new business to become a full-time job.

Word of Mouth

Millan's first clients were dogs belonging to some of his employer's friends. His employer admired Millan's uncanny ability to work with difficult dogs, and he was not shy about recommending him to friends with difficult dogs. "He'd call up his friends and say, 'I've got this great Mexican guy who's amazing with dogs. Just bring 'em over,'"[49] Millan says—and they did.

"Tcccchhhh"

Millan always tells clients that they should never, ever strike or kick a dog. When he is working with a dog, he uses a few "tools" to bring a dog's focus back to the business at hand. For example, when he has the dog sitting but can tell it is distracted by a passing human or dog, Millan may reach his leg around and tap the dog's hindquarters with his toe. In some cases, he may use his hand in the same way a mother dog corrects her pups. He makes his hand into a "C" shape, and gently pokes the dog. He explains that his hand is like the mouth, and his fingers are like the teeth. Again, it is only a reminder to pay attention, and he never does it to hurt or punish a dog.

But perhaps his signature correction is a sound, a "Tcccchhhh!" noise that he often uses in combination with other corrections. He tells clients he learned it from his mother. When he or his siblings were misbehaving she would use that noise to let them know she disapproved. It seems to work just as well with misbehaving dogs.

Not surprisingly, his early customers were Doberman pinschers and Rottweilers. As he evaluated them, he continued to apply his ideas about what the dogs needed to be happy. Perhaps most important, he realized, was that the dogs on his grandfather's farm had had plenty of exercise. Because dogs in the wild are always moving, always migrating, he knew that it was vital for dogs to have plenty of exercise each day.

By using a few of the more balanced dogs he had been working with to help rehabilitate the newer, unbalanced dogs, Millan began walking his "pack" all at once. His English had improved a little in the time he had been in the United States—enough to communicate with his customers. But he never had any trouble communicating with the dogs. Eventually, in fact, he was walking a pack of seven Dobermans and two Rottweilers—a spectacle that people in the area had never seen. His visibility with those dogs was also the best advertisement for his new business. "People would see me with my pack," says Millan, "and they'd think, if that guy can control thirty dogs, he can help me with mine."[50]

And just as he had hoped, over the coming months his business became so successful that he was able to quit his job washing limousines and devote his full energy to rehabilitating dogs. He was happy and energized doing what he loved to do—and what seemed like second nature to him.

"Okay, Let's Get This Straight"

One day in 1994 he met another of his "guardian angels"—individuals who reached out a hand to help him, asking nothing in return. At that time he was at a client's home rehabilitating a Rottweiler named Kanji. The owner had strong connections to the entertainment industry, and like the limousine company's owner, had been spreading the word about how good Millan was with troubled dogs.

That day a woman came to the house with a Rottweiler puppy—one of Kanji's puppies, as it turned out. She asked Millan if he would be willing to train her dog, and he agreed. She looked familiar to him, but he could not figure out why. They set a time three weeks away, when he would come to her home to begin training the dog.

The day of their appointment, he rang the doorbell, and was dumbfounded when actor Will Smith answered the door. The woman he had spoken to was Smith's wife, actress Jada Pinkett Smith. He recalls thinking, "Okay, let's get this straight: I'm in America for only three or four years, I now have my own successful business, and today I'm working with Jada Pinkett and Will Smith's dog?"[51]

In addition to the puppy he had already seen, the couple had two new dogs, given to them by the host of *The Tonight Show*, Jay Leno. All three of the dogs would need work, so he eagerly got busy. He was pleased that Jada was interested in his methods and seemed to pick up quickly on the idea of calm energy and leadership. But Jada was also interested in helping Millan. She introduced him to many other friends who owned dogs—dogs that she was sure would benefit from his help. She also became a person Millan could turn to in the months and years ahead as he became more well known. Having been around Hollywood, she seemed to have a sixth sense about whom he could trust and what offers were too good to be true. Not surprisingly, he considers her a great friend. "Jada has been more than my client," he says. "She's been my mentor, my sister, and another one of my precious guardian angels."[52]

"For Me, It's About Respect for This Country"

But one of the most treasured gifts Jada Pinkett Smith gave him was a teacher. She could see that while Millan was immensely talented, his limited English would hold him back. To make sure that did not happen, she hired a private tutor for a whole year to help him learn English. She knew that as he became more in demand, he could be as good at communicating with people as he was with their dogs.

The English lessons opened up a whole new world for Millan. He began reading books he'd never heard of before—books

One of Millan's first clients was actress Jada Pinkett Smith, who was so impressed with his methods that she referred him to several of her friends who owned dogs.

"Our Chuck E. Cheese"

In his article "What the Dog Saw," *New Yorker* writer Malcolm Gladwell describes a favorite playtime activity in the Millan's Dog Psychology Center and notes the pinpoint control Millan has with the dogs.

> Beyond the Dog Psychology Center, between the back fence and the walls of the adjoining buildings, Cesar has built a dog run—a stretch of grass and dirt as long as a city block. "This is our Chuck E. Cheese," Cesar said. . . . Cesar had a bag over his shoulder, filled with tennis balls, and a long orange plastic ball scoop in his right hand. He reached into the bag with the scoop, grabbed a tennis ball, and flung it in a smooth practiced motion off the wall of an adjoining warehouse. A dozen dogs set off in ragged pursuit. Cesar wheeled and threw another ball, in the opposite direction, and then a third, and then a fourth. . . . "The game should be played five or ten minutes, maybe fifteen minutes," Cesar said. . . . With that, Cesar gathered himself, stood stock still, and let out a short whistle. . . . Suddenly there was absolute quiet. All forty-seven dogs stopped charging and jumping and stood [as] still as Cesar, their heads erect, eyes trained on their ringleader. Cesar nodded . . . toward the enclosure, and all forty-seven dogs turned and filed happily back through the gate.

Malcolm Gladwell, "What the Dog Saw," *New Yorker*, May 22, 2006, p. 48.

on animal behavior, dog psychology, and a range of other subjects. "I began a program of self-education," he says, "reading everything I could get my hands on."[53]

He says that he approached learning English—not an easy language—in the same way he approached learning any new job. "I threw myself into learning English," he says.

> As I said before, I'm a perfectionist. I credit my mom for a lot of that, especially when it comes to speaking correctly.

She provided a strong foundation for me. She had wanted to be a teacher, but became a full-time mom instead. But she always insisted that we speak Spanish correctly at home. Good grammar, no incomplete sentences—she would correct us if we spoke that way.[54]

But he feels another reason for his drive was not just to learn English, but to master it with the English lessons Jada Pinkett Smith provided for him.

The question is, why do I speak English well, when so many others like me who jumped [crossed the border illegally] don't speak it at all, or speak it poorly? They don't try to really engage. Language is important, and knowing it shows a respect for my new home. Just like President Obama—he's very important, but tries to greet people around the world in their language. It's like he's saying, "I'm a human being who wants to engage with you, at least I can greet you in your language." For me, it's about respect for this country, and the people here.[55]

Meeting Ilusion

During the time his business was expanding, Millan had begun dating a young woman named Ilusion. "I first met her at an ice skating place in L.A.," he remembers.

I'd gotten a call from this girl I knew that she and her friend needed a ride. That was strange—seeing ice for the first time. Growing up in Mexico, and living in L.A., I'd never seen snow or ice, but there were people skating around. Anyway, the friend turned out to be Ilusion—she was just doing her little thing out on the ice, back and forth, back and forth, which I found fascinating."[56]

Did he know she was "the one"? "No, no," he says, laughing. "If you asked Ilusion, she'll tell you that she knew right away about us, but not me. Remember, I went because I wanted to date the other girl, the one who called me."[57]

Millan and Ilusion married when she was eighteen. Early
on, the couple experienced rough times because of their
cultural differences but with therapy have kept their
marriage strong.

They did begin dating, but Millan soon learned something that scared him. A friend told him that in the United States it was against the law for him to be dating Ilusion because she was only sixteen. Frightened that he could be arrested and deported back to Mexico, he quickly ended the relationship, which was sad for both of them. However, the day she turned eighteen, Ilusion came back into his life. That same year, they married, and Ilusion was expecting their first child.

A Rough Start

Ilusion soon became very unhappy, however, and for a while it seemed as though their marriage would not last. She says now she was very frustrated with Millan, for he seemed far more interested in his dog than his marriage. Even after the baby was born—a son, whom they named Andre—Millan seemed to be much more in tune with his dogs' needs than those of his wife.

A large part of the problem, she soon realized, was that he had a different view of marriage than she did. "His view was that marriage was where a man tells a woman what to do," she remembers. "Never give affection. Never give compassion or understanding. Marriage is about keeping the man happy, and that's where it ends."[58]

Eventually Ilusion left with Andre. She told Millan that their marriage was over unless he would agree to counseling. Today, Millan recalls saying that he would try counseling, although he was doubtful that he needed any help. He did not think he had anything to learn. But he was wrong.

Through therapy, Ilusion says, she and Cesar realized that much of the problem was a cultural thing. In traditional Mexican marriages, the husband's and wife's roles are very clear. He makes decisions, and she obeys. That is the way he was brought up, and that is the model he had for being a husband. But through counseling, he realized that he needed to be as understanding of Ilusion's needs as he was of his dogs' needs. And that realization not only saved their marriage, it gave him an insight that would be invaluable in his business, too. For a man who had never connected with people as well as with dogs, it was an inspiration. "[I]t was the moment when he understood that to succeed in the world, he could not just be a dog whisperer," says Ilusion. "He needed to be a people whisperer."[59]

Millan agrees, saying simply, "Ilusion rehabilitated me in the same way I rehabilitate unbalanced dogs. She made me see what a gift a strong partner and family is, and that every member of a family needs to pull his or her own weight."[60]

Chapter 4

The Dog Whisperer Begins

As Cesar and Ilusion were working on strengthening their marriage, it was clear that some changes needed to happen with his business, too. Millan had a lot of clients whose dogs needed rehabilitating. But rescue organizations were also pleading with him to rehabilitate some of their hard-to-place dogs that otherwise might have to be euthanized. These dogs would need a place to stay, and he could not keep them in his studio apartment. His dog business needed more space—and soon.

Millan rented a run-down building on two acres of land in the warehouse district of South Los Angeles, an area near the turf of several L.A. gangs. When he began using it to house a large number of big, powerful dogs that he would take on runs through the neighborhood, it is no wonder that crime statistics in the area went down quickly.

A Home for the Pack

Millan named the facility the Dog Psychology Center, which he described as "sort of a permanent halfway house or 'group therapy' drop-in station for dogs."[61] Anywhere between thirty and fifty dogs would stay at this center—some permanently or until they were adopted, others temporarily while they were rehabilitated. Some had medical issues that made them unacceptable to their owners.

Many of the dogs had been abused or neglected. Some were pit bulls who had been used for illegal dogfights. In many cases,

Millan started the Dog Psychology Center in East Los Angeles as a place to house all the dogs that he was training. Between thirty and fifty dogs stayed at the Center and most of them had been neglected and abused.

a dog that loses an important fight or becomes injured so it is of no use to the owners is simply abandoned to fend for itself on the streets. Popeye is one of those dogs. He had lost an eye in a dogfight, and because of his limited vision he was nervous and aggressive around other dogs and humans.

Another pit bull, Rosemary, had been severely injured after losing a fight; her owners had doused her with gasoline and set her on fire. After she was rescued and her burns had healed, she was aggressive and frightened of people. Millan worked patiently with dogs like Popeye and Rosemary, rehabilitating them to become happy, balanced members of his pack.

One of the most beloved of the pack was Daddy, a pit bull who was once owned by a rap artist named Redman. Redman was a good owner and brought Daddy to the Dog Psychology Center because he needed his dog to be calm and easygoing. "I need a dog I can take anywhere in the world with me," Redman told Millan. "I don't want a lawsuit."[62] Daddy eventually became a permanent member of the pack when Redman, who was so often on the road, gave him to Millan.

In the fourteen years that he had been part of the Dog Psychology Center, Daddy was an ambassador for his breed, demonstrating to people how mellow and easygoing a pit bull can be with the right care. "Everyone who meets him falls in love with him," Millan says, "even though on the outside he is very formidable. Daddy has helped hundreds of dogs become balanced, simply by sharing his calm-submissive energy."[63]

Exercise and More Exercise

From the beginning, Millan began a routine for his pack that reinforced his role as pack leader and was helpful in the dogs' rehabilitation. One thing he knew for certain was that the pack needed exercise. It makes no difference if a dog is a purebred or a mixed breed that lives on a Mexican farm or in a busy city like New York or Los Angeles; exercise is a daily necessity.

Dog owners who think a ten-minute walk around the block is sufficient exercise for a dog would be quite surprised at the level of exercise Millan provides his pack. He and an assistant would load the dogs into a large van by 6:00 A.M. and drive toward the Santa Monica Mountains. The dogs were unloaded at the foothills and began a four-hour exercise session, as Cesar explained:

On this typical route, we walk to the top, which takes an hour. We stop at a lake, where the dogs cool down. They swim, they relax. After 30 minutes we walk for another hour. We enter a wooded area, where I allow them to relieve themselves in the trees. They have exactly five minutes to come back for formation. I walk again for an hour, and they follow. A pack leader doesn't have to talk. When he moves, so does his pack."[64]

Millan keeps a steady, quick pace of about 3.5 miles per hour—a speed that will burn off energy but allow the dogs to keep moving for a long period of time. He puts backpacks on the larger dogs, so that when one of the little dogs gets tired, it can ride. All of the dogs are off-leash for their morning walk. If a dog at the

Exercise was a necessity for Millan's "pack," which typically consisted of German shepherds, rottweilers, and pit bulls. He would walk, hike, or rollerblade with the dogs every day in and around Los Angeles.

center is still having problems becoming part of the pack, it stays home, and one of Millan's assistants exercises it there.

A Sudden Spotlight

Several times in Millan's life people took notice of his unusual gift of communicating with dogs. However, none was as important as a newspaper article that was published in the *Los Angeles*

Times in 2002. Written by Bettijane Levine, the article, called "Redeeming Rover," was the first media profile of Millan and his methods.

The article talked about Millan's strong belief that even the most difficult, aggressive, and troubled dogs can be rehabilitated if they are approached in the right way. Levine interviewed one of Millan's clients, Leslie Rankin, whose coonhound Elvis had bitten people so often that Rankin was no longer able to have guests visit her at home. Elvis stayed at the Dog Psychology Center for five weeks, Rankin says, and when he came home, he was totally changed.

"Like Prozac, but without the Side Effects"

During season two of *The Dog Whisperer*, Millan worked with a dog named Nugget, who had been adopted from the dog pound by Russ and Nancy Briley. He was a loveable, happy dog, but soon developed a strange habit of eating (not just chewing) odd things. He ate wood, plastic soccer cones, carpeting, and dish towels. Once a vet had to perform emergency surgery on the dog when he ate part of the family's trampoline.

When they admitted to Millan that they were walking Nugget only three times a week, he knew that was a big part of the problem. "When a dog destroys a house and chew[s] things, it's just like a physical exercise," he explained. "When you get a dog that is a working type and don't have any activity to share, it develops issues, like the one you have. . . . Walking is like Prozac, but without the side effects."

He taught them both how to control Nugget's energy on the walk so it was enjoyable, and soon Nugget had stopped his odd eating altogether, much to everyone's amazement.

Quoted in Jim Milio and Melissa Jo Peltier, *Dog Whisperer with Cesar Millan: The Ultimate Episode Guide.* New York: Fireside, 2008, p. 191.

"He's happy. He likes people. He knows how to play with other dogs," she told the reporter. "People are no longer afraid of him. . . . Cesar was able to break through to the Elvis that I knew was inside."[65]

A Hollywood Buzz

The article had an amazing effect, creating a buzz of excitement in Hollywood. Within days, hordes of television producers were making their way to the Dog Psychology Center to see Millan first-hand, hoping to sign him up to do a reality show. And he lived up to their expectations—with his good looks, likeable personality, and positive approach, he would almost certainly be a hit.

Millan liked the idea of appearing on television and getting his message across to more people than he could ever reach in person. He quickly chose two lesser-known producers, Kay Sumner and Sheila Emery—an easy choice, he says, because they had no interest in changing anything about him or his methods for television.

Sumner and Emery offered the idea to two cable channels— Animal Planet and the National Geographic Network. A show about rehabilitating dogs would fit with either, but National Geographic gave them the best deal, taking a chance by ordering twenty-six thirty-minute episodes of *The Dog Whisperer with Cesar Millan* for the 2004–2005 season. Each show would feature Millan meeting people with problem dogs and showing the owners how to eliminate those problems.

Real Reality Television

The producers knew it would be important for viewers to watch Millan in action rehabilitating dogs. It could not be staged, or fake—and it would be fake if he observed any of the problem dogs before taping the show. So the producers put ads in local newspapers, seeking dog owners who were having serious issues with their pets. To sift through the responses, they held an audition at which Sumner, Emery, and Ilusion Millan could see the dogs and assess the level of their problem.

The Dog Whisperer with Cesar Millan features Millan meeting people with problem dogs and showing the owners how to eliminate those problems. Millan is strict in that the show is "real" without anything being staged or fake.

Once they had chosen a case, the production team would go to the house to film the owners and their dog, documenting the type of misbehavior. When that part of the taping was finished, Millan himself would go to the house, introduce himself, and ask how he could help. *Dog Whisperer* executive producers Jim Milio and Melissa Jo Peltier say that it is all very real. "Cesar knows nothing about the dogs or owners he is about to meet, and the crew truly never knows where Cesar—or the dogs—are going to go or what they're going to do next."[66]

Most viewers do not have any idea that retakes, or do-overs, are not permitted when Millan is working with a dog—and that is Millan's own rule. "[The dogs] don't understand 'take two,'"[67] he explains. For example, if a dog bites him and draws blood, it appears in the show. And when the usually positive and enthusiastic Millan becomes frustrated while working with a woman who seems to be favoring her dog over her child, that appears in the show, too. In fact, not only are such parts kept in—they actually make the show more interesting to viewers. "That's actually what got me to watch the show," says Marli, a New York viewer.

> Me—I love it when Cesar gets kind of moved by the people he meets, like he gets a little teary. Or when the dog doesn't always respond right away, and you can kind of tell Cesar is surprised, like, hey—this is a bigger challenge— and he likes that. It makes him and the show seem real. I normally hate reality shows, because they're so fake, you know? But you can tell Cesar is real. I don't even have a dog, and I watch the show.[68]

Small Budget, Big Reaction

The Dog Whisperer with Cesar Millan debuted on September 13, 2004, at 6:30 P.M. on the National Geographic Channel. Because the debut would not be shown during prime time, it had not been promoted by the channel. No one could predict how successful it would be.

The first episode got fairly good ratings. But they were nothing compared to the ratings of episodes that aired in the following weeks. While the National Geographic Channel did not advertise the show, people who had stumbled across it while channel surfing were amazed. They told others about the almost mystical way that even the most ill-behaved dogs would respond to Millan, and as a result, the audience for the program grew quickly.

The number of viewers increased even more when Millan was featured on some of the most popular network shows, such as *Oprah* and *The Tonight Show*. In the months that followed, it was clear that *The Dog Whisperer with Cesar Millan* was on its way to becoming the most popular of all the shows on National Geographic. A second season was ordered, then a third. It won Emmy nominations for best reality TV program in 2006, 2007, and 2008. The ratings have continued to climb, and by March 2009, National Geographic announced that it had renewed the show for a sixth season.

Praise and Tears

The program's message has continued to resonate with viewers. Millan knew it was important to give the television viewers information that would help them as much as the dog owners featured on the show. At the heart of each program was the philosophy that he had come to rely on—that all dogs need a strong, calm leader. People who hit or scream at their dogs are not good leaders, nor are people who interact with their dogs only by pampering them.

He believes people want to do the right thing by their dogs, but they do not realize that it is leadership—rather than love and affection—which is the dog's primary need. "What a dog calls love is not what we give," he says. "If a dog is okay with just love, I would not be in business. Americans know how to love better than anybody else. This is the country that will throw a birthday party for a dog, and spend $15,000 to $20,000 [in vet bills] on a dog to get cured."[69]

Leadership, he says, means being calm, assertive, and providing the dog with practice, or discipline, in behaving the way the leader wants the dog to behave. Just as dogs follow a strong, confident pack leader in the wild, they follow a human leader who shows those qualities. And with practice, any owner can become a leader, no matter how old or how physically strong that person is.

The message has gotten through to many dog owners. Connie Diaz, a Texas teacher, says she has changed her whole approach to living with her dog, a four-year-old Dalmatian named Dwight who was driving her crazy chewing the furniture:

> I watched Cesar explaining to a woman on the show that her dog got no exercise, and that's why he was being destructive and aggressive," she says. "And he might as well have been talking to me. I started that very evening walking Dwight, and haven't let a day go by since, without walking him—and it's made all the difference. Dwight is a happier, more content dog, and he's not tearing the sofa cushions apart and eating the furniture like he used to.[70]

Millan believes that it is leadership, rather than love and affection, that is a dog's primary need.

"I Wish He'd Gotten His Show Sooner"

One of the most often-heard remarks by viewers is that they wish they had known before what they have learned from the show. Gilian Roth, a teacher from Minneapolis, says that when she watches *The Dog Whisperer*, she is both intrigued and sad. "Cesar makes so much sense, on so many levels," she says. "And when he works with the dangerous dogs—the red-zone cases, he calls them—I've never heard him say, 'That dog needs to be put down,' or 'This dog is too dangerous to be around people.'"[71]

Roth says that she is still mourning the loss of a stray dog she had adopted named Pete. She had him for three years, but when he began biting people, she was told by her veterinarian that euthanizing Pete was the only answer.

"I think about Pete all the time," she says.

> But especially when I watch Cesar's show. I think I was three or four episodes into *The Dog Whisperer* when I watched Cesar rehabilitate a biting dog, and I said to myself, "That's Pete." Cesar knows just what to do, and he's helped so many dogs that were ten times worse than Pete become happy and social again. And it just makes me so sad that no one I talked to back then gave me any ideas of what to do, any solutions, any hope at all. I wish I'd known about Cesar back when Pete was still alive.[72]

Critics Speak Out

But not all of the response to Millan's show has been as positive. Some dog trainers insist his methods could be dangerous for owners who try his methods themselves. They point to one approach he uses when an aggressive dog makes a threatening move toward another dog. Millan will sometimes quickly put the aggressor on its side in a submissive position until the dog understands it needs to become calm. "I have a client right now who did a lot of the stuff he [does on the show]. . . . And lo and behold, the dog caused fifty stitches in her face,"[73] says one New York dog trainer.

Feeding the Pack

In *A Member of the Family*, the Millans' younger son Calvin talks about helping feed the dogs at the Dog Psychology Center. As he explains, there is a lot more to it than pouring food into a dish.

> At the Center, my dad also taught us how to feed the dogs. You gather the food and you put in the dish with your hands and you mix it up well. Then you call the dogs, and my dad has a special way of holding the plate up in the air. And he holds the plate up until the dogs sit back and look at him and then he holds it up again, so he makes them wait. Then when they're sitting down, he puts the dish down and he does it to every dog except for Daddy, because [D]addy is pretty old now and gets special food. Daddy gets this raw meat, and it's cold so we have it in the freezer.

Quoted in Cesar Millan, *A Member of the Family*. New York, Harmony, 2008, p. 260.

Millan taught his young son Calvin a special way to feed the dogs at the Dog Psychology Center.

Another complains that Millan has no training in dog behavior and therefore has no credentials. "When you have experts with PhDs who disagree with him, why have we Americans chosen to follow this unschooled guy?" complains the editor of *Bark* magazine. "He says he learned everything by observing dogs on a farm. Is this how you become an expert?"[74]

But his defenders—many of whom are veterinarians, rescue organizations, and dog trainers, reject such criticism. They think criticism may be fueled by jealousy because of the fame and attention Millan has received. As far as his methods being dangerous, supporters point out that the show clearly warns viewers not to try Millan's methods of dealing with aggressive "red-zone" dogs. Such a warning appears at the beginning of each episode, urging viewers to seek a professional's help instead.

Many dog professionals such as Milwaukee dog trainer Amy Ammen says Millan has raised awareness about dog training, enabling people to be more informed and savvy about what type of training they want for their dogs. She says her clients are very interested in knowing if the class will use Cesar's methods. "My clients mention him over and over and over," she says. "Now people are motivated to pick up the phone and ask about him. They ask, 'How Cesar is the class?' This is a good thing. They have a basis of comparison, and they also have hope."[75]

Millan himself is unfazed by the criticism. "That is the beauty of America. People can say what they want," he says. "I don't see things that way. I'm bringing back common sense, as far as I'm concerned. There are 68 million dogs in America, and they need help. I'm helping them. I'm saving lives."[76]

Chapter 5

Lessons from Dogs

Since the premiere of *The Dog Whisperer*, Millan's popularity has steadily increased. Not only has his show continued to do extremely well, but he has also expanded his reach in helping dog owners. With the help of writer Melissa Jo Peltier he wrote *Cesar's Way*, a book chronicling his life in Mexico and fulfilling his dream of coming to the United States.

That book was followed by two more: *Be the Pack Leader* and *A Member of the Family*, which detail ways that dog owners can establish leadership with their dogs. All three have topped the *New York Times* best-seller list, and a fourth book, *How to Raise the Perfect Dog*, was released in October 2009. But while his successes have made him wealthy and influential, he is unwilling to merely lie back and enjoy life.

Tackling the Hard Issues

One of the many benefits of success is the chance it can give a person to achieve other goals. For many years Millan has been saddened by the large number of dogs that are euthanized in the United States. Of course, euthanasia can be a humane way to put a very sick or severely injured animal out of its misery. However, in far too many cases, it is used to kill millions of healthy dogs, simply because too many of them are in shelters across the country.

A group of fans line up outside a Petco store in Miami, Florida, waiting to meet Millan and get copies of his book signed.

In May 2009 Millan traveled to San Antonio, Texas, for an event called "Dog Awareness Week." San Antonio has one of the highest rates of euthanasia in the United States—since the beginning of that year, five thousand dogs had already been euthanized. One of the problems is that so many dog owners in San Antonio do not get their pets spayed or neutered. As a result, too many dogs are without homes, and overcrowded and underfunded shelters have no options other than to euthanize them.

While in San Antonio, Millan did public service announcements in both Spanish and English (the city is predominantly Hispanic). He urged people to work toward the city's goal of reducing the number of dogs in shelters. If people would spay and neuter their dogs, he said, shelters could become "no-kill" facilities—meaning they would never have to resort to euthanasia. The goal for San Antonio was to have a no-kill policy by the year 2012.

Organizers of the event were pleased that Millan came to San Antonio and used his popularity for such a good cause. Said one, "We're hoping that the community will really listen to him."[77]

Taking on Puppy Mills

The euthanasia issue is just one aspect of a much larger problem, Millan says. He knows that overcrowded shelters are due in part to people choosing to buy expensive purebred dogs from breeders on the Internet or from pet stores and not from an American Kennel Club–approved breeder. Dogs from unlicensed breeders and pet stores are very likely to come from a puppy mill—a type of breeding facility that the Humane Society has been trying to wipe out in the United States.

Simply put, puppy mills throughout the United States churn out more than one million purebred puppies each year, born to females that are forced to become pregnant over and over. They live their entire lives in tiny wire cages, deprived of human companionship, kindness, and even the most basic medical care. Once the females are too old or sick to have another litter, they are killed or abandoned.

The puppies are sold to pet stores around the country or on the Internet. Because they are cute, they are hard for unknowing dog

Officials rescue dogs from a puppy mill in Virginia that had six hundred breeding females. Millan urges his viewers to adopt from a local shelter or rescue group instead of a puppy mill.

lovers to resist. However, experts warn that puppies from puppy mills are far more likely to have serious genetic diseases and disorders, as well as eye and skin problems. And because they are crowded into small cages and do not interact with people early in life, they tend to be difficult to socialize.

"I Felt a Lot of Frustration"

During the 2008 season of *The Dog Whisperer*, Cesar went undercover with a dog rescue group called Last Chance for Animals, or LCA. Using hidden cameras, Millan and two LCA workers were able to take viewers inside a puppy mill to witness firsthand the horrible conditions there.

Millan said later it was hard not to be angry when he saw so much misery:"It takes a lot of concentration not to judge [puppy mill owners] when you know they're doing something wrong. But in order for me to help and influence them, I have to see what they're doing. I saw a dog that was blind. I saw many dogs in one kennel. I felt a lot of frustration; I felt a lot of confusion . . . definitely aggression . . . a lot of anxiety."[78]

Millan and the LCA workers were able to negotiate with the owner of the puppy mill to take eleven of the breeder dogs, which were no longer of any use to him. Millan explained that the LCA workers took care of the physical and medical needs of the rescued dogs, while his job was to teach those workers how to care for the dogs' psychological needs after being caged for so many years. The experience moved him, and he urged viewers, "When you bring a dog into your life, please do your homework and don't buy a dog from a puppy mill. Visit a local shelter or rescue group instead."[79]

Changes at the Dog Psychology Center

Millan's life is undergoing other changes in addition to the expansion of locations and topics on his show. One of the most exciting for him is the creation of a new Dog Psychology Center.

"I have always had this dream of a bigger Center," he said in July 2009. "I envisioned a place with lots of green space for

the dogs to roam, a place for them to swim. And it is coming true. We are shutting down the DPC in south L.A.—something that is sad in a way, because it was how we started off in rehabilitating the pack." But now, he says, he and Ilusion were able to buy property in the Santa Clarita Valley, less than 50 miles (80.5km) northwest of downtown Los Angeles. "Instead of two acres in the city, we now have 42 acres in the country," he says. "No smog, the air is clean and beautiful. And we're going to put a lake in, for the dogs to swim. The traffic is terrible, but we like listening to music, so we do that while we're waiting in traffic."[80]

Millan moved his Dog Psychology Center from downtown Los Angeles (pictured here) to the Santa Clarita Valley where the dogs live on a 42-acre compound.

"Oh, Dad, We've Heard this Story Before"

In addition to having more space for a larger number of dogs, Millan and his family can live on the property to be closer to the pack. He says that the new DPC is a dream that he has been thinking about for a long time. "Dreaming is important—planning, making lists, having intentions," he says. "I believe you have to think about the power of having a dream. But part of it is being patient, too." Millan says that he sees that so many people are not patient today. They don't like to wait, and when they have to, they become annoyed. "Society today is 'Now! Give it to me now!'" he says. "We live in a world of microwaves. Hey, I come from a place where you've got to bring the wood and prepare the wood and wait until the fire gets red, and then it's ready to put the meat on. That's where I'm from."[81]

He insists that he is not complaining about his upbringing in Mexico; in fact, he says, learning to be patient has helped him. "I think [having to wait] was a good thing. There was more of a rhythm to life, you were waiting for the food to cook, sure, but your family had more time to be together. That's a process, and it gave you appreciation. Speed is great, of course, but the fire was good in a lot of other ways."[82]

As he thinks back about his days in Mexico cooking on a fire, Millan laughs. "I talk about this stuff to my boys [Andre and Calvin] all the time," he says. "I'm like an old man, telling stories about the past. I've been doing this ever since they were little—even before they could understand—I'd talk to them about their great-grandfather and things like that. They'd just stare at me, mesmerized by my conversation." He talks a lot about life on the farm, and some of the things he has accomplished in the years since then. "I tell them where I'm from, how I met famous people. When one of the boys complains, 'Oh, Dad, we've heard this story before,' the other one says, 'Be quiet! That's our great-grandfather he's talking about—that's where our dad learned what he knows.'"[83]

"I'm Very Lucky"

It is easy to see that family—his human pack—is the most important thing in Millan's life. "I'm very lucky," he says.

> I have an amazing, smart wife who loves me, and two wonderful boys. I love watching them grow. We try to keep them balanced—it's important that they don't get all caught

up in the world of fame, of Hollywood, of television, you know? We don't expose them to a lot of it. But at the same time, I want them to know that anything is possible if you work hard, if you're honest, and have a very high level of integrity.[84]

He is proud of both of his sons, saying they work very hard for everything they have. "It's kind of a combination of the United States and Mexico," he says. "They have the awareness of the United States, but have the learnings of Mexico. We're very family oriented; family is first with us. My boys know that if they are going to do something, they think about how it will impact our family," he says. "Is it going to be a healthy impact, or a negative impact? That way, hopefully, they are conscious of the idea of 'think before you act.' But I couldn't be prouder of them both."[85]

A Dog for Andre

The Millans' older son, Andre, had wanted a dog of his own for a long time. The one he ended up with was not one his father would have recommended. It was Apollo, a Rottweiler that had bitten many people and was slated to be euthanized at a shelter when Cesar Millan agreed to work with him.

Andre came into the garage when I was working with [Apollo] and I was worried. He is good with dogs, but I wasn't sure about Apollo, and I didn't want him to get bitten. But it was an amazing moment—there was just something magical between them. It is both good and bad, in my memory. Good because there were no cameras there, so it is just a memory between Andre and me. Bad because I was still concerned. But it was clear, the trust between them—I don't know another way to say it other than it was divine.

Cesar Millan, telephone interview by author, July 14, 2009.

Amazing Things

Though he turned forty in August 2009, Millan is able to look back on some amazing things that he has experienced—especially in the years since he came from Mexico. One was finding out that astronaut Sunita Williams is one of his fans—and has actually watched episodes of *The Dog Whisperer* while in space.

Williams has a Jack Russell terrier that she missed a lot while on her mission, which launched in December 2007. Since she had to spend six months on the International Space Station, she told Millan that she brought along a copy of his first book, *Cesar's Way*. She also arranged to receive episodes of his show on weekly uplinks.

American astronaut Sunita Williams read Millan's book Cesar's Way *while in space and corresponded with him via satellite.*

Millan says it was a very humbling experience to be able to speak via satellite with Williams while she was in space:

> The two things I enjoyed most were seeing Earth from her window—what an amazing view—and being able to share the experience with my son Andre. He has expressed an interest in one day following in Suni's footsteps and becoming an astronomer. . . . I really admire people who go to outer space. They put their lives on the line to do research which benefits humankind.[86]

"I Am an American Man"

But perhaps no experience has made him prouder than the ceremony that took place on March 12, 2009. On that day Millan, alongside dozens of other immigrants, took the oath to become an American citizen. On his Web site that morning he was clearly excited about the coming event. "Today I officially become an American citizen, and I could not be more proud!"[87] he wrote.

He knows his life has been, in a very real way, the spirit of the American dream: starting small, working hard, and becoming a success. "Immigrants such as myself come to the United States because of the opportunities available here. You are free to be the person you choose to be spiritually, emotionally, and intellectually," he writes. "The sky is the limit!"[88]

He knows that millions of others in Mexico and other places people are too poor to bribe officials to get visas to allow them to come to the United States. He is also aware that people in the United States have varied opinions about how the immigration issue should be handled. "I think immigration is a serious issue, and I am glad that is being debated in this country," he says. "I hope someday the resolution will allow people like me with a dream and a desire to come to America and do so legally."[89]

Paying It Forward

Millan believes that people should use their gifts to make the world a better place. He knows he has been lucky to achieve so

Millan at a 2009 pet adoption event. He has stated that as an American he is excited about new opportunities and making a difference in the lives of dogs and people.

much success, and he is excited about more opportunities to make a difference. "Not just for my family, not just for me," he says. "America is my fatherland now; whatever I can do for this country I will do it. I'm an American man now. So that to me is a great thing."[90]

He feels that each person makes a difference in his or her own way. "I do think I can make a difference through dogs," he says. "It's kind of a metaphor—but I don't want anyone to think I'm just using dogs to make a point, or to take advantage of them. I'm not. It's just that dogs are special. They highlight things. For some reason, people become more open minded when we talk about dogs." He pauses a moment, thinking. "I'll give you an example," he says. "Dogs can make people of different races forget race, and just be human first, rather than Caucasian, black, Asian, Mexican, whatever. You put those people in one room and they talk about race, there's going to be a disagreement, right? But you put those people in the same room and talk about their dogs, and there's going to be a whole different atmosphere. That's the way it is. That's just the way it is."[91]

Reconnecting

Millan believes that dogs are also one of the closest links people have to nature, and that gives them even more importance. "At one point, early on, people were connected to nature," he says. "We took cues from the sky, the birds, the wind. And then we became very intelligent, and then making money and using technology became more important. That's when we lost that connection, I think."[92]

Dogs can teach people so many things, he says.

For me, they remind me that life is best when it is lived in the moment. I tell people that dogs don't think about things that happened before, or worry about what is going to happen in the future. That's the beauty of dogs, but it's something we humans don't have. I could be worrying about things—I try not to. I mean, there are business things that I could start to be nervous about, worry about,

Daddy and Junior

A strong supporter of pit bulls, Millan feels it is important that he always have one as part of his pack to offset the negative stereotype people have about the breed. For that reason, when a vet technician invited him to his house to see some new pit bull puppies, Millan agreed and brought Daddy along. One pup caught his eye—a gray one with powder-blue eyes. "Though he didn't resemble Daddy physically," Millan wrote later, "his energy made me feel as if I were going back in time and seeing Daddy again when he was a puppy. In my heart, I heard myself saying, 'That's him. That's the one.'"

Daddy, too, was attracted to the puppy, and that sealed the deal for Millan. The puppy is named Junior, and he is growing into a smart, balanced dog. It seems certain that Junior will be the next pit bull ambassador in Cesar's pack.

In February 2010, Daddy, the remarkable pit bull who had been Millan's right-hand man in rehabilitating many dogs, passed away. In fact, in the sixteen years that Millan had

Daddy, he says they had reached the level in their friendship at which they could instinctively read one another's thoughts.

Quoted in Cesar Millan, *A Member of the Family*. New York: Harmony, 2008, p. 79.

Millan and his pit bull Daddy pose at an event.

but I don't. That's one thing I've learned from dogs—they've taught me that. And I don't want to let my teachers down by not using their advice![93]

One thing that Millan knows for sure is that he is happiest when he is around dogs. He still is up by 6:00 A.M. every morning to hike for four hours with his pack, just as he did when he first started the Dog Psychology Center in Los Angeles. In fact, he says, he can't imagine fame ever changing that routine.

"I see fame the way my dogs see fame. It's not real," he says. "I am the same Mexican guy who jumped the border with a dream. Only with better clothes."[94]

Introduction: Needing Help

1. Quoted in "The Wrath of Opie," *Dog Whisperer with Cesar Millan—The Complete First Season*, video, MPH Entertainment, 2006.

2. Quoted in "One Last Chance," *Dog Whisperer with Cesar Millan—The Complete First Season*, video, MPH Entertainment, 2006.

3. Quoted in Jim Milio and Melissa Jo Peltier, *Dog Whisperer with Cesar Millan: The Ultimate Episode Guide.* New York: Fireside, 2008, p. 9.

4. Quoted in "The Wrath of Opie."

5. Quoted in "One Last Chance."

Chapter 1: *El Perrero*

6. Cesar Millan, *Cesar's Way.* New York: Harmony, 2006, p. 24.

7. Millan, *Cesar's Way*, pp. 21–22.

8. Millan, *Cesar's Way*, p. 21.

9. Millan, *Cesar's Way*, p. 22.

10. Millan, *Cesar's Way*, p. 24.

11. Millan, *Cesar's Way*, p. 27.

12. Millan, *Cesar's Way*, p. 28.

13. Millan, *Cesar's Way*, p. 31.

14. Millan, *Cesar's Way*, p. 30.

15. Millan, *Cesar's Way*, pp. 30–31.

16. Millan, *Cesar's Way*, p. 32.

17. Millan, *Cesar's Way*, p. 33.

18. Millan, *Cesar's Way*, p. 52.

19. Millan, *Cesar's Way*, p. 34.

20. Cesar Millan, telephone interview by the author, July14, 2009.

21. Millan, *Cesar's Way*, p. 31.

22. Millan, telephone interview by the author, July 14, 2009.

23. Millan, telephone interview by the author, July 14, 2009.

24. Millan, *Cesar's Way*, p. 34.

Chapter 2: Beginnings of a Dream

25. Millan, *Cesar's Way*, p. 35.
26. Quoted in Edward Wyatt, "A 'Whisperer' Howl of Triumph from the Curb Up," *New York Times*, May 23, 2006, p. E1.
27. Millan, *Cesar's Way*, p. 36.
28. Quoted in Mary-Jo Dionne, "Cesar Millan: The Man behind the Whisper," Modern Dog Online. www.moderndogmagazine .com/articles/cesar-millan/755.
29. Quoted in Cesar Millan, "How Things Have Changed," *Cesar Speaks*, January 31, 2009. www.cesarmillaninc.com/edit orials/editorial_32.php.
30. Quoted in Dionne, "Cesar Millan."
31. Millan, telephone interview by the author, July 14, 2009.
32. Millan, *Cesar's Way*, pp. 36–37.
33. Millan, *Cesar's Way*, p. 38.
34. Millan, telephone interview by the author, July 14, 2009.
35. Millan, telephone interview by the author, July 14, 2009.
36. Quoted in Dionne, "Cesar Millan."
37. Millan, *Cesar's Way*, p. 39.
38. Quoted in Lucy Cavendish, "Leader of the Pack Pet Subjects," *Sunday Telegraph*, March 2, 2008, p. 18.
39. Millan, *Cesar's Way*, pp. 42–43.
40. Millan, *Cesar's Way*, p. 43.
41. Millan, *Cesar's Way*, p. 43.

Chapter 3: Breaking Away

42. Millan, *Cesar's Way*, p. viii.
43. Millan, *Cesar's Way*, p. 45.
44. Millan, *Cesar's Way*, p. 46.
45. Millan, *Cesar's Way*, p. 47.
46. Millan, *Cesar's Way*, p. 47.
47. Millan, *Cesar's Way*, p. 48.
48. Quoted in Mimi Avins, "A Sage for the Canine Set," *Los Angeles Times*, October 18, 2004, p. E1.
49. Millan, *Cesar's Way*, p. 49.
50. Quoted in Avins, "A Sage for the Canine Set," p. E2.
51. Millan, *Cesar's Way*, p. 52.
52. Millan, *Cesar's Way*, p. 53.

53. Millan, *Cesar's Way*, p. 53.

54. Millan, telephone interview by the author, July 14, 2009.

55. Millan, telephone interview by the author, July 14, 2009.

56. Millan, telephone interview by the author, July 14, 2009.

57. Millan, telephone interview by the author, July 14, 2009.

58. Quoted in Malcolm Gladwell, "What the Dog Saw," *New Yorker*, May 22, 2006, p. 48.

59. Quoted in Gladwell, "What the Dog Saw," p. 48.

60. Millan, *Cesar's Way*, p. 54.

Chapter 4: *The Dog Whisperer* Begins

61. Millan, *Cesar's Way*, p. 54.

62. Quoted in Millan, *Cesar's Way*, p. 127.

63. Millan, *Cesar's Way*, p. 127.

64. Quoted in Bettijane Levine, "Redeeming Rover," *Los Angeles Times*, September 25, 2002, p. E1.

65. Quoted in Levine, "Redeeming Rover," p. E1.

66. Milio and Peltier, *Dog Whisperer*, p. xx.

67. Quoted in Milio and Peltier, *Dog Whisperer*, p. xx.

68. Cesar Millan, telephone interview by the author, July 31, 2009.

69. Quoted in Morieka V. Johnson, "Q & A: Cesar Millan," *Atlanta Journal-Constitution*, April 3, 2006, p. C1.

70. Connie, telephone interview by the author, July 18, 2009.

71. Gilian, personal interview by the author, Minneapolis, Minnesota, August 1, 2009.

72. Gilian, personal interview by the author, August 1, 2009.

73. Quoted in Denise Flaim, "Bad Doggie Medicine?" *Chicago Tribune*, May 23, 2006, p. 1.

74. Quoted in Sanjiv Bhattacharya, "Leader of the Pack," *Ottawa Citizen*, March 25, 2007, p. B4.

75. Quoted in Jackie Loohauis, "The Sound and the Furry," *Milwaukee Journal Sentinel*, June 13, 2006, p. E1.

76. Quoted in Loohauis, "The Sound and the Furry," p. E1.

Chapter 5: Lessons from Dogs

77. Quoted in Brian Chasnoff, "'Whisperer' Is Ready to Speak Out," *San Antonio Express-News*, May 29, 2009, p. B1.

78. Quoted in *Monsters and Critics*, "Dog Whisperer Cesar Millan Takes on Puppy Mills." www.monstersandcritics.com/smallscreen/features/article_1475925.php/Dog_Whisperer_Cesar_Millan_takes_on_Puppy_Mills_Friday_May_8.

79. Quoted in *Monsters and Critics*, "Dog Whisperer Cesar Millan Takes on Puppy Mills."

80. Millan, telephone interview by the author, July 14, 2009.

81. Millan, telephone interview by the author, July 14, 2009.

82. Millan, telephone interview by the author, July 14, 2009.

83. Millan, telephone interview by the author, July 14, 2009.

84. Millan, telephone interview by the author, July 14, 2009.

85. Millan, telephone interview by the author, July 14, 2009.

86. Cesar Millan, "My Biggest Fan in Space!" *Cesar Speaks*, August 2007. www.cesarmillaninc.com/editorials/editorial_12.php.

87. Cesar Millan, "Proud to Be an American!" *Cesar Speaks*, March 2009. www.cesarmillaninc.com/editorials/editorial_35.php.

88. Quoted in Joanna Poncavage, "'Dog Whisperer' Speaks Up About Success," *Morning Call* (Allentown, PA), July 30, 2006, p. E1.

89. Millan, telephone interview by the author, July 14, 2009.

90. Millan, telephone interview by the author, July 14, 2009.

91. Millan, telephone interview by the author, July 14, 2009.

92. Millan, telephone interview by the author, July 14, 2009.

93. Millan, telephone interview by the author, July 14, 2009.

94. Quoted in Dionne, "Cesar Millan."

For Further Reading

Books

Bruce Fogle, *The Dog's Mind: Understanding Your Dog's Behavior*. New York: Macmillan, 1992. Though an older book, this is one of the first dog psychology books Millan read when he became proficient enough in English. He says it is one of the main books that influenced him.

Jim Milio and Melissa Jo Peltier, *Dog Whisperer with Cesar Millan: The Ultimate Episode Guide*. New York: Fireside, 2008. A must for anyone who enjoys Millan's television show, this book details each of the first three seasons' episodes and gives interesting behind-the-scenes information, as well as updates on how the dogs are doing now.

Cesar Millan, *Cesar's Way: The Natural, Everyday Guide to Understanding & Correcting Common Dog Problems*. New York: Harmony, 2006. Lots of good details about his early years in Mexico.

Cesar Millan, *A Member of the Family: Cesar Millan's Guide to a Lifetime of Fulfillment with Your Dog*. New York: Harmony, 2008. Includes two fun chapters, each written by one of his two sons. Also, good information about choosing the right dog.

Periodicals

Malcolm Gladwell, "What the Dog Saw," *New Yorker*, May 22, 2006.

Sharon Peters, "The Snarls Don't Faze Trainer," *USA Today*, May 31, 2007.

Edward Wyatt, "A 'Whisperer' Howl of Triumph from the Curb Up," *New York Times*, May 23, 2006.

Web Sites

American Society for the Prevention of Cruelty to Animals (www.aspca.org). The ASPCA is one of the world's most influential organizations dedicated to the welfare of animals.

The Web site offers tips on helping animals, ways to contribute in one's own community, and interesting articles that deal with rescues of abused or homeless animals.

Cesar Millan Kids (www.cesarmillankids.com). Created by Calvin Millan, Cesar's younger son, the Web site is great for even younger readers. It includes games, monthly contests, and information about the relationship between kids and dogs.

Cesar's Way (www.cesarsway.com). This Web site offers extensive information on dog behavior, with quizzes and fun facts and a monthly letter from Millan about something new that is happening with him or his pack.

Millan, Ilusion, 53, *54*, 63
  on Cesar's view of marriage,
    55

N
Nugget (dog), 62

O
Opie (black Lab mix), 8, 11
Oprah, 65

P
Pacific Point Canine
  Academy, 46
Peltier, Melissa Jo, 64, 71
Pit bulls, 57–59
Popeye (pit bull), 58, 59
Puppy mills, 73, *74*, 75

R
Rankin, Leslie, 62–63

Red zone cases, 38, 68, 70
Redman (rap artist), 39
Rosemary (pit bull), 59
Roth, Gilian, 68
Rottweiler, 49, 79

S
Saluki (Irish setter), 23, 24
San Antonio (TX), 73
Smith, Jada Pinkett, 50, *51*
Smith, Will, 50
Sumner, Kay, 63

T
Therapy, 55
Tijuana, 33–35, *34*
The Tonight Show, 50, 65

W
Williams, Sunita, *80*, 80–81
Wyatt, Edward, 38

Gail B. Stewart is the author of more than 250 books for children and young adults. She lives with her husband in Minneapolis, and they have three grown sons. While Stewart really enjoyed speaking extensively with Cesar Millan, it has not resulted in any dramatic change in the behavior of her own dogs, unfortunately.